ADAM SANDLER
Not Too Shabby

ADAM SANDLER
Not Too Shabby

An Unauthorized biography

BY JON SALEM

SCHOLASTIC INC.

New York Toronto London Auckland Sydney
Mexico City New Delhi Hong Kong

Photo credits

Front Cover: Bonnie Schiffman/Outline
Back Cover: Stephan Danelian/Outline

ISBN 0-439-10427-0

12 11 10 9 8 7 6 5 4 3 2   9/9 0 1 2 3 4/0

Printed in the U.S.A.

First Scholastic printing, June 1999

Acknowledgments

My sincere appreciation to those who thoughtfully shared with me their wonderful memories and impressions of Adam Sandler: Michael Clemons, Tamra Davis, Mel Gordon, Lucien Hold, Chris Kendall, Barry Moss, Robert Schiavone, Melanie Sprouse, and Richie Tienken.

My thanks to Christina Ferrari of *Teen People* and Glenn Kenny of *Premiere* for their insightful views on Adam Sandler's career and popularity.

My gratitude to the Eudora Welty Library, Amy Galleazzi, Stephanie Hauck, Peter Kendall, Manchester High School Central, Holly Millea, Betsy Nolan, Matt Robinson, Jim Salem, Judy Savage, Janet Scott, Tom Scott III, Barbara Seaman, Mark Shuttleworth, Mrs. Spiro, the University of Alabama's Gorgas Library, the *Volusian Daytona Beach News Journal*, Webster Elementary School, Ronald Williamson, and Jeremy Zimmer for invaluable assistance.

Special thanks to Kitty Kelley for providing the inspiration to pursue biographies.

A bow to my editor, Randi Reisfeld, for her guidance, enthusiasm, and thoughtful direction.

And finally to Linda Konner, my agent, whose solid support and confidence means so very much.

This book is dedicated with love to my mother, Donna Salem. In the words of Adam, she's "not too shabby!"

Contents

Prologue: The Sandman's Revenge   1

1. Reading, Writing, and In-School Suspension   5

2. A Lesson from Bill Cosby   15

3. It's Saturday Night!   26

4. Back to the Principal's Office   35

5. Don't Worry, Be Happy   42

6. A Little Music, a Little Romance   46

7. Phi Beta Sandler   56

8. Splish Splash   62

9. The Big Daddy of Comedy   71

Epilogue: Last Laugh   80

Appendix: The Essential Adam Collection   84

Prologue:
The Sandman's
Revenge

**Adam always was very ambitious. People just kind
of accepted that he was going to be as big as he is.**
— Tim Herlihy, close friend and coscreenwriter

It was the day that a mama's boy called Bobby
Boucher from the cajun bayou shocked Hollywood — Monday, November 9, 1998. Opening-weekend box-office returns for Adam Sandler's
The Waterboy were in, and the final tally — $39
million — exceeded all expectations.

"I didn't think it was going to be that huge,"
Glenn Kenny, film critic and senior editor of the
movie magazine *Premiere*, admits. "I thought
maybe eighteen or twenty million."

Just like his on-screen persona Bobby Boucher,
Adam Sandler was underestimated. He steam-rolled over the competition, hitting hard and
without mercy. The first to get body slammed
was Jim Carrey, whose *Ace Ventura: When Na-*

ture Calls lost its first-place position as the movie with the highest three-day ticket sales for a nonsummer release. And the tackles didn't stop there. Brad Pitt got it next. His holiday release *Meet Joe Black* didn't stand a chance against *The Waterboy*. Even the screaming kids of *I Still Know What You Did Last Summer* couldn't scare Adam to a stop. In just 17 days, his movie sailed past the $100-million box-office mark.

Adam Sandler was already a *star*, but within the 72 hours it took *The Waterboy* to drink in those megabucks he became a *superstar.* "Adam is one of our top-ten most requested celebrities," says Christina Ferrari, managing editor of *Teen People*. "*The Waterboy* really lifted him up into a whole new category of popularity. He was not a teen idol before, but he definitely is now."

One person who's less than pleased about Adam's success is Isabel Pellarin, a teacher at his alma mater, New Hampshire's Manchester High School Central. "I can't believe he's making all that money for things he was being punished for here," she noted to a *People* correspondent.

When he bagged a win for "The Star Who Leaves Us Laughing" in the first annual *Teen People* Readers' Choice Awards, he claimed the top slot by a healthy margin. In fact, 41 percent of the first-weekend audience for *The Waterboy* was under 17, a youth rally that forced Hollywood to show Adam some respect.

"The paradox of the movie business is that it chases young filmgoers, but it's not run by them," observes Mr. Kenny, *Premiere*'s film critic. "The industry didn't understand Adam Sandler, and they weren't prepared for his success. Now they'll take him more seriously."

The Hollywood hotshots are wising up already. One had this to say in *The New York Times*: "Adam has a link to the psyche of an awful lot of people. It has something to do with his vulnerability. People identify with him."

Millions of people. And for a 32-year-old class clown whose very own college drama department advised him to *give up* acting, recognition like that is, well, *not too shabby*. Same goes for the story behind his success. His personal journey contains the very elements that make his movies so popular:

a zany character to cheer for
naysayers who eat their words
big laughs
nick-of-time triumph
and lots of heart

But this time out the hero isn't Billy, Happy, Robbie, Bobby, or even Operaman. It's Adam. Adam Sandler. His friends call him The Sandman, and he's the hottest comedian in the business.

Just the way he planned it.

Living the Life of Adam Tip #1

Is your mom mad at you? Try this trick: When she's scolding you, secretly tape record her and then play it back. Chances are she'll start to laugh and forget about your being in trouble at all. That's what happened when Adam pulled the same stunt on his mom!

1
Reading, Writing, and In-School Suspension

Adam was just like Bart Simpson.
— Michael Clemons, Manchester High School Central

Born to Stan and Judy Sandler on September 6, 1966, Adam is the youngest of four. His older sibs are brother Scott and sisters Elizabeth and Valerie. The family relocated from Brooklyn, New York, to Manchester, New Hampshire, just in time for Adam's first-grade debut. A new neighborhood and new school is a tough adjustment for any kid, and Adam was no exception. But unlike most young tykes at the age of six, Adam lived by his own rules.

On his first day of first grade at Webster Elementary, when all the other children dashed outside for recess, Adam quietly gathered up his lunchbox and walked home. His teacher, Mrs. Chris Kendall, remembers the day well. Because he was new to the school, he hadn't come up from preschool with the kindergarten class, so he probably thought the day was over. "His mom brought him back and all was fine."

Until the next day . . . when Adam pulled the same early exit all over again. "I called his mother and asked, 'Is Adam there?' Sure enough, he was hiding in the bushes," Mrs. Kendall laughs. "His first couple days of school were real teary-eyed."

The mad dashes home became a regular routine. After asking permission to be excused, Adam would be out the door, up the hill, and into his kitchen for a peanut butter and jelly sandwich, reported *Entertainment Weekly*. And then his mother would see him safely back to school.

Gradually, the fear of a new place subsided, and Adam began to relax and have fun. "He enjoyed humor," Mrs. Kendall says. "He just enjoyed life. He always helped people and liked to have a good laugh."

Even his teacher's husband, Peter Kendall, has crystal-clear memories of Adam. While on a shopping excursion at Service Merchandise that year, the couple ran into Adam and his mother. "Back then I had a mustache and sideburns, and Sonny and Cher were quite popular," Mr. Kendall recalls. A few days later, the encounter turned up in a cute story by the first grader. "HE'S

FUNNY, HE LOOKS LIKE SONNY," Adam wrote.

"He was a cutup," Mr. Kendall says. "He was quite a kid."

The pint-sized poet also demonstrated an early gift for song. At seven, Adam was crooning "The Candy Man" for local nursing-home residents and, by his mother's special request, "Maria" from the stage hit *West Side Story*. "He'd keep her happy most of the time," older brother Scott recalled to *People*.

Adam didn't just work overtime for laughs. Like most young boys, he tried to do sports, too. At eight, he entered a neighborhood Punt, Pass, and Kick tournament and took the top prize — but not because of future NFL possibilities. "I was the only kid in my age bracket," he confessed to his mother. "I wanted to pretend that I was the champion but it was really because I was the only kid there." He didn't fare much better in baseball. "I was slow," he remarked to *E-Online*. "I was the only kid in Little League who could hit one to the wall and get thrown out at first base."

But Judy Sandler didn't mind. The thoughtful homemaker and her engineer husband Stan raised a loving and close-knit family. Adam's first-grade teacher remembers Judy Sandler well. Mrs. Kendall was set to get married the summer after Adam graduated. She was touched when Adam's mom decided to throw her a classroom kitchen shower as a way for the kids to celebrate their teacher's pending nuptials. The children brought small items like potato peelers, and they even made their own cards, which, amusingly, came emblazoned with the phrase HAPPY WETTING DAY. Good bet that Adam had a hand in that project!

Stan Sandler, now retired, is a kind soul, too. "My dad was twenty when he started having a family, and he was always the coolest dad," Adam told pal Ben Stiller during a rap session for *Interview*. "He did everything for his kids, and he never made us feel like he was pressured." "Everything" included help with wild Halloween costumes. Adam has one all-time favorite. "My dad made me a cape. It was red on the inside and zebra on the outside. It was kind of a Lenny Kravitz Dracula," he told *Entertainment Weekly*. Growing up in such a supportive environment gave Adam the security to pursue his own interests, no matter how silly they may have been.

"Until sixth grade, I did really well in school. All of a sudden, I said, 'I can't read and be so serious in class anymore.' I don't know why, but I just started goofing off. I decided to have fun," Adam revealed to *Mademoiselle*. The fun started with his first stage gig — singing at his sister's wedding. "I sang 'You're Sixteen.' It was the only song I knew all the words to," he told *People*. His first number got an enthusiastic response, so he performed another, Paul McCartney's "Yesterday," . . . which didn't. "Everyone was like, 'Get off, you're not that good.'" And *this* was twenty years before *The Wedding Singer*!

Adam's older brother Scott became a lawyer, his sister Elizabeth a dentist, and Valerie a food industry executive. Of course, Adam didn't fare so badly either, but the early signs of success were difficult to pinpoint.

Michael Clemons, then a U.S. government teacher at Manchester High School Central, remembers the teenage Adam. "He was an underachiever. He could have done anything that he wanted as far as academics were concerned, but they weren't his concern."

Adam was no poster child for Career Day, but he was always charming. "Every day, I used to look forward to the class Adam was in," Mr. Clemons admits, "even though he was a pain. But he was very funny. Just when I was ready to put my hands around his throat and strangle him, he'd look up at me and say, 'You know, Mr. Clemons, you're my favorite teacher.' And I'd start laughing. We have a lot of kids who try to be class clowns, but he was good at it. You got mad at Adam, but he could disarm you and change your mood."

Robert Schiavone, now principal of Central but a guidance counselor when Adam attended in the early eighties, remembers him as "Detention Boy." "I would have to try and bail him out of all this trouble he'd get in and keep a straight face in the process." One of the funnier scenarios was Adam's in-school suspension. The disciplinary action is designed to keep students quiet and focused on class work for an entire day. To Adam, it sounded like a plan to watch his favorite TV shows. He showed up packing a fluffy pillow and a portable TV!

"He was sent out of class much more than others, but it wasn't for things harmful to people," Mr. Schiavone says. "Adam did things that were mischievous and fun-loving. They were against school rules most of the time, but they were creative!"

When he wasn't riding around with friends, Adam played in a rock band. At one time or another the group called themselves Spectrum, Storm, and Final Warning (which shows up as the name of a band in *The Wedding Singer*). In fact, before comedy claimed him, Adam dreamed first of being a rock singer. He even organized a local Battle of the Bands competition that was held in the Central auditorium.

It's a well-worn cliché that rock stars get the girls. Perhaps Adam thought his status as a music man would help him win the favor of senior class beauty Linda St. Martin. "Adam used to come in every day and say, 'Linda, when are you going to go out with me?'" Mr. Clemons says. "Linda would turn to him and say, 'Adam, not until hell freezes over.' This became a daily routine. Now I think of Adam's success and wonder if Linda regrets it."

Approaching the prettiest girl wasn't his only brave move. "If I was dared to [moon] the cafeteria, I wouldn't even think twice," he told *Mademoiselle*. This unpredictable side is one reason why Mr. Clemons seated him next to the door. "So I could throw him out easily!"

Well, at least his peers liked him. "He was popular," Mr. Schiavone says. "The students always invited him to whatever they were doing because they wanted to see what *he* was going to do." He did enough to share "Class Clown" honors with three other students during his senior year.

Despite his less than successful attempts at football and baseball as a kid, Adam loved sports and played junior varsity basketball in high school. He also dabbled in politics, serving as a student-council delegate. In school and out, Adam moved in a tight clique of kids that included athletes and school newspaper scribes, among others. But most of all, Adam had a good time and got involved.

Although humor has always been Adam's way

of relating to people, sometimes he's used it to laugh away the pain. As he confessed to *Mademoiselle*, "I was always a little bit of an outsider. Everywhere I went I heard comments about being Jewish. And it would hurt." Of course, years later he would transform that pain into a radio-friendly comedy hit with "The Chanukah Song." The lyrics, about being the only kid in town without a Christmas tree, are more than just silly rhymes.

Being the target of anti-Semitic jokes, or any ridicule rooted in hatred and ignorance, is a painful experience that lingers. For Adam, the sting may be there even today, but his own comedy has never been fueled by pain. *Teen People*'s Christina Ferrari believes that's the reason teenage fans respond to him so strongly. "Adam's not trying to be over anybody's head, too cool, or cynical. He's not making fun of other people. He makes fun of himself more than anybody. For teenagers, that's very important. They're very sensitive and don't like it when people make fun of them, so comedy based on that doesn't work as well."

Although the jibes at Adam's expense stirred up hurt feelings, he never indulged in self-pity. After all, that kind of attitude never left an audience rolling in the aisles. He cracked up his dad by memorizing Rodney Dangerfield routines and had his mom doubling over with an on-the-spot impression of his dad's loud sneeze. "He's always been funny; he always woke up in a good mood," his mom told *Entertainment Weekly*. "We knew he would be an entertainer. The only person who minded was Grandma Anna. She'd ask him, 'Why can't you be a funny doctor?'"

Adam's teacher Mr. Clemons wasn't sure about his career intentions, either. "I told him once, 'There are five million comedians in the United States out of work. Why don't you try to choose another field?' But he told me — and I remember this like it was yesterday — 'I'm going to be a comedian.'"

Clearly by high school, Adam knew exactly what he wanted to do, but it was only after the urging of his brother that he put the plan into serious motion. Scott was attending Boston University and scouting open-mike nights at area comedy clubs when he encouraged his younger sibling to go for it. Adam recalled to Ben Stiller in *Interview*, "If [Scott] hadn't said to do it, I wouldn't have thought it was a normal thing to do. I would have said, 'Mom and Dad are going to get mad at me.' But I knew that my parents respected his brain. I was like — he said to do it, so it must be okay."

At 17, Adam headed for the future . . . in the concrete jungle of New York City.

Living the
Life of Adam
Tip #2

Do you have a favorite T-shirt or sweatshirt?
Write a song about it. Adam's ditty "Red Hooded
Sweatshirt" includes the words "dip dip dip,"
and "shama lama ding dong." Remember, to be
funny Adam-style, it doesn't have to make
sense!

2
A Lesson from Bill Cosby

When I saw Adam, I just believed right off the bat that this kid was something special.
— *Lucien Hold, the Comic Strip's talent coordinator*

Performing a stand-up comedy routine looked easy, but it turned out to be more difficult than cracking jokes in Mr. Clemons' U.S. government class. In fact, Adam's first gig at Boston's Stitches Comedy Club was no laughing matter. "I remember going onstage, not knowing what to say, and hearing some guy slurring, 'He's got a retainer,'" he recalled to *Entertainment Weekly*.

But Adam soldiered on, and the summer between high school graduation and college freshman year further developed his hunger for success. For the first time, Adam got serious about the business of being funny. "I said, 'Okay, this is what I want to do,'" he admitted to *USA Today*. "Then I made the decision, 'Oh, man, I gotta get on *Saturday Night Live.*'"

The first step toward getting there was New York University (NYU), where Adam enrolled to study acting at the acclaimed Lee Strasberg Studio. For cash he tried working as a waiter (got fired), pharmacy clerk (got fired), and a New York subway street musician (did okay).

NYU is not known for having a clubby school spirit. Most universities have sprawling greens and a home-away-from-home college-life atmosphere, but NYU's "campus" is part of a neighborhood called the East Village. Unlike the way it's depicted on *Felicity,* for the thousands of students enrolled, it's survival of the fittest. That's especially true of the acting school, one of the more competitive programs. "I was kind of lost, so I just did what they told me to do," Adam posted during an *E-Online* chat. "I don't remember paying enough attention when I was there. If I had to do it all over again, I'd definitely pay more attention."

A man named Mel Gordon was Adam's student advisor during the NYU years. Here's what he remembers: "Focus and concentration — that's the thing Adam was lacking the most. He was always looking out the window. He didn't take anything seriously. Thinking of him reminds me of Jeremy Piven (TV's *Ellen* and *Cupid*), the *most* inattentive student I can remember. Jeremy's very similar to Adam — likable and irritating at the same time."

His acting teachers focused in on the irritating. "Naturally, they didn't like him because he was the character he plays now," Mr. Gordon says. But the disdain went even deeper — the drama department wanted him *out* altogether! NYU's acting program is similar to graduate school in that high grades are expected. In theory, getting a C is like failing a major, so each year the professors would assemble a list of students who needed "the talk." Of course, Adam Sandler made the cut. The talk, in fact, meant you'd better rethink your career plans.

Yet Adam paid no attention. "He wasn't interpreting the message in the way that I wanted," Mr. Gordon remembers. Adam's laid-back attitude toward acting school courted the dislike of his teachers, but, amazingly, this fueled his desire to make it big. "I think that disapproval was a great inspiration," Mr. Gordon says. "Adam had tremendous will and managed to invent a place for himself, so I admire him a lot. I think he's great."

Years later, Adam and Mel Gordon enjoyed a chance encounter at a Hollywood restaurant. Adam, at the peak of his *Saturday Night Live* success, was developing *Billy Madison* and came sauntering in with superstar Brad Pitt and character actor Steve Buscemi. "Adam sees me," Mel recalls, "and he comes running over, saying 'Mel Gordon, Mel Gordon, Mel Gordon.' Then he calls Brad and Steve over. He was very excited to see me. The only thing he remembers is that I was the only faculty member who talked nicely to him at NYU."

Adam made his mark in college as a prankster, too. In his dorm, he would blast Led Zeppelin tunes and shout "Hey, you!" to pedestrians from his window. "It was funny to pick on random people," roommate Tim Herlihy told *People*. In short order, the two became friends. "I couldn't believe the stuff coming out of his mouth. It's the stuff we think but don't say," Tim once remarked.

When Adam decided it was time to take on the New York comedy circuit, Tim got involved and wrote his friend a few bits. Adam thought the routines were solid, and the guys have written together ever since, collaborating on *Billy Madison*, *Happy Gilmore*, *The Waterboy*, plus songs and other stand-up material.

Another NYU pal was Lorenzo Quinn, son of movie legend Anthony Quinn. Lorenzo suggested that Adam talk to his father, and the elder and more famous Quinn arranged for Adam to meet with Bill Cosby, who at that point ruled Thursday night television with *The Cosby Show*. Generously, Bill asked Adam to perform an example from his comedy act. Reluctantly, Adam launched into one of his funnier raunchy bits. But Bill Cosby didn't laugh. He merely stared and said, "You can't do that. You're not going to get anywhere with that stuff."

Bill Cosby's advice to do clean comedy was taken to heart, and soon Adam was ready for one of New York's most prestigious clubs, the Comic Strip. In fact, a nine-o'clock slot on Saturday night at the Comic Strip is the spot of choice in the game of comedy. Since 1976, this showcase club has been a training ground for the hottest comedians in the business. Jerry Seinfeld, Eddie Murphy, Paul Reiser, Chris Rock, and Ray Romano all earned their stand-up merit badges there, and it's a stage they always come back to. Even today, before tours or guest spots on Jay Leno and David Letterman, the top names still hit the Comic Strip to work out material.

Lucien Hold is the club's talent coordinator and one of the first New York star makers who took an interest in Adam. "He was only nineteen, and I signed him up immediately," Mr. Hold says. "He had all clean stuff — very quirky, very cute. I thought, this guy is really good. The next day I got a phone call from Adam thanking me for being so kind. For the longest time he would call regularly, almost every day."

Adam's impressive audition prompted Mr. Hold to alert a man named Richie Tienken, one of the Comic Strip's owners who once managed Eddie Murphy. Mr. Tienken shared Mr. Hold's admiration. "Adam had a quality about him," he says, "a very likable quality. His stand-up on its own, with somebody else doing it, wouldn't have been funny. But Adam had a way of getting it across. I just felt that people would like him. That got me interested."

Another manager, Barry Moss of Hughes Moss Casting, was hooked as well. "I remember seeing him do stand-up when somebody heckled him," Mr. Moss says. "Adam came back with something so good-naturedly funny and really won me over at that point. He was very compelling. He had a real star quality that I was almost alone in seeing in the beginning."

Instantly, a pivotal triangle was formed to accelerate Adam's career. Lucien Hold stood dedicated to see Adam capture the coveted Saturday night slot at the Comic Strip, while Richie Tienken and Barry Moss teamed up to manage his career. Being cast as a regular on *Saturday Night Live* was the ultimate goal, but until then it was important to raise Adam's profile. As the casting director for *The Cosby Show*, Mr. Moss helped sign Adam to the recurring role of Smitty, Theo Huxtable's oddball friend. It was a part created specifically for him. Adam played Smitty with his trademark quirky charm, and his interactions with Bill Cosby's Cliff Huxtable character are a hoot to watch.

The Cosby Show was Adam's first TV gig, but it wasn't his only one. He enjoyed sidekick status on *Remote Control*, the MTV game show that featured college-age contestants flexing their memory muscles on TV trivia — all in the name of prizes. Colin Quinn (now on *Saturday Night Live*) and Denis Leary worked alongside Adam at this baby-step moment in their careers.

Through it all, Adam never lost sight of his first goal — to join the cast of *Saturday Night Live*. The best shot at getting there was a brilliant stand-up audition, but every screen credit would help. Adam nabbed a small role in a feature film, 1989's *Going Overboard*. The movie faded fast, but it cemented Adam's belief that movies were his ultimate future. "There were two things that Adam really wanted," Mr. Moss recalls. "To be a movie star and to make records." *Saturday Night Live* was the best boot camp for both, so Adam worked hard to set himself up for that opportunity.

Between TV, movie projects, and a successful appearance on *Showtime at the Apollo*, Adam worked exclusively for the Comic Strip, almost on a nightly basis. It took him just one year to nab the Saturday night slot that is every comedian's dream of all dreams. But Adam's aspirations extended far beyond stand-up success. "He never really wanted to be a great stand-up comedian," Mr. Tienken says. "I think he wanted to do what he's doing now — movies. Jerry Seinfeld wanted to be the best stand-up comedian there ever was. He told me that twenty years ago. I don't think Adam cared about it enough. That was just a way of getting up in front of an audience and being able to get the gratification that performers need."

Mr. Moss adds, "Adam was inconsistent in his stand-up. He wasn't always brilliant. In fact, he was *less* than brilliant more often than he was. Basically, he would just wing it. He wouldn't plan anything."

Adam's lack of preparation worked for *and* against him. "The bottom line is, Adam never really had an act. It was him. It was his personality. He had some bits that were very funny, though not enough to sustain laughs for an entire set. Even at his best, he would bomb a little bit. But that's part of Adam's quality," says Mr. Hold of the Comic Strip.

So is a pigpen approach to writing. No one could ever accuse Adam of excessive neatness. He shrugs off computers to scribble his stand-up material on scratch paper, napkins, and magazines. "They're just beat-up, really old, and all smudged, with the tiniest writing," he explained to *Mademoiselle*.

Of those early routines, three remain memorable. There's a bit he used to do about his grandmother, who lost hearing in both ears, yet put two hearing aids in one ear — which gave her "bionic listening power" in that one and total deafness in the other! A second routine joked about living in a cul-de-sac at the bottom of a hill during icy winter storms. Cars couldn't drive up the hill, but pizza delivery guys could drive down it. By the end of the freeze, the Sandlers would have eight or more pizza drivers sleeping in the living room! There was also a gag about a little Elvis Presley that lived in Adam's refrigerator. When he opened the door, the King would talk to him, and Adam would yell, "Shut up!" There's not much of a point to that routine. It's just Adam being silly.

Unlike many comics who work out inner demons through their acts and use the stage as a form of therapy, Adam's routines have no subtext. They're just plain goofy. "He's one of the happiest people who happens to be a comic," Mr. Hold says. "Most [comedians] are very moody and dour — not Adam."

Even when he bombed, Adam knew how to turn things around. "No matter what, audiences liked him," Mr. Tienken says. "That's a big part of stand-up. If the crowd likes you, you can get by." Mr. Hold recalls another talent that helped Adam survive nights with few laughs. "When a joke doesn't work, a lot of comics blame the audience. Adam never did that. It was always his fault. He's very self-effacing, and that's a key to his success."

This winning attitude accelerated Adam's ride to *Saturday Night Live*. "He came along pretty fast," Mr. Hold remembers. So fast that Adam took off for Los Angeles to try his luck at the West Coast version of the Comic Strip — The Improv. Rumor has it that acid-tongued comic Dennis Miller caught his act and dropped a suggestion to *Saturday Night Live* producer Lorne Michaels that the weekly variety show should scoop him up. But that's not the way his big break really came about. He got there the hard way — with one this-is-your-moment chance to show his stuff to the people who mattered.

His managers secured Adam an official *Saturday Night Live* audition, which meant the program's scouts would come to the club, check out his act, and render a decision. Given Adam's hot/cold stage reputation, the prospect was daunting. In the world of comedy, every stand-up wants to hear the words, "You killed them!" And that's exactly what Adam needed. The opportunity of a lifetime was riding on one routine.

Living the
Life of Adam
Tip #3

Do you think you'll be famous one day? Then take your picture to the busiest restaurant in town and tell the owner to tack it up. That's what Adam did to John Stratidis at New York's famous Cozy Soup 'n' Burger on Eighth Street and Broadway. Be bold!

3
It's Saturday Night!

Adam said he was going to be gigantic. He always thought he was going to be a big comedy star.
— Richie Tienken, former manager

"I made him sit down and write out exactly what he was going to say, an outline of his act for that night," Barry Moss recalls of the *Saturday Night Live* audition. This time, the preparation worked. "He was incredible. It might have been the best stand-up that Adam's ever done." In essence, he killed them, and an offer to join the show — as a *writer* — hit the table. It was 1990.

That proved to be a real stepping-stone. For after putting in one year as a writer, Adam graduated to featured-player status. The first week of his promotion is one he remembers well. Tom Hanks was guest host, and Adam was scared to death. He recalled the night to a freelance writer.

"Ten seconds before the lights come up on my first skit, I say to Tom, 'I might faint. There is a good chance I'm going to faint.' Hanks looks over, real concerned, and says, 'Well, don't.'" And Adam didn't. There was too much at stake.

In the business of comedy, Adam worked overtime. "It's the only thing that I think about," he told the *Chicago Tribune*, "the only thing that I pour all my energy into. I don't know why I do it; it just happens that that's what goes through my head." He definitely needed a brain like that for *Saturday Night Live*, a comedy institution known to hit meteoric highs and pitiful lows in the span of its 90-minute airtime.

The first "Live, from New York, it's Saturday night!" exclamation was uttered October 11, 1975, when Adam was just nine years old. George Carlin hosted, mixing it up with a cast that included comic greats Dan Aykroyd, John Belushi, Chevy Chase, Jane Curtin, and Gilda Radner.

Since its inaugural airing almost a quarter of a century ago, *Saturday Night Live* hasn't altered its format. There's the opening skit with the shouted introduction, a monologue from a superstar guest host, comedy sketches, commercial parodies, two numbers from a hot musical act, and a final ensemble shot of all the players hugging each other as they sign off.

The show's six-day incubation period from creation to broadcast played to Adam's strengths.

As a key sketch player who wrote his own routines, he lived and breathed *Saturday Night Live*, putting in countless hours, often working until 6:00 A.M. and starting all over again that same afternoon. The demands of a live show are incredibly intense, as Adam shared with Ben Stiller for *Interview*. "Doing *Saturday Night Live* definitely affects my relationship with my family because you feel so much pressure to do well that night. But I think everyone's grown to accept that, so they give me my space at the show."

Adam whooped it up with a talented cast that included David Spade, Rob Schneider, Chris Rock, Mike Myers, and Chris Farley. Even with that hilarious group skits sometimes fell flat, but Adam let *Seventeen* in on the group's quick recovery method. "You make eye contact with the guy you're bombing with and you just share the moment. You lose a little sleep over it, but the next week you try to do better." Not much sleep was lost for lack of comedic success. Adam's signature characters gave the show a surge of excitement, and studio 8-H, where the series has been taped since the first airing, rocked with laughter each week.

The real work on an episode of *Saturday Night Live* starts on Monday, when sketch ideas are pitched and writers begin to structure the show. On Tuesday, scribes like Adam work overtime while a 250-person production crew rockets into action. There are sets to assemble, costumes to design, music to compose and record, and movie star hosts to pamper and prepare for the live variety format.

By Wednesday, the show begins to get organized. The cast, crew, and guest host meet in a large conference room to read through about 35 sketch ideas. Besides the show itself, this meeting is do-or-die. Only about 11 skits get the green light, so there's a competitive edge in the air. After all, every performer and writer wants his or her stuff to be selected.

Things heat up at Thursday's rewrite sessions, where rough sketches are scratched and scribbled into finished drafts. This process often turns into an all-nighter. Fridays are just as jazzy because all concerned are preparing for the next day's dress rehearsal, which ends only one hour before the actual show begins. There are always more sketches included in the dress rehearsal than can be accommodated once the program goes live. The ones that play weakly — usually about three — are dropped at the last minute.

After the final stage good-bye to the studio audience (lucky holders of hard-to-get tickets), everybody heads to a Manhattan hot spot for the weekly cast party, another typical all-nighter.

Adam's top priority was to make the most of

his *Saturday Night Live* opportunity. Getting sketches on the air week after week was a tough order that required hard work and strategy. Eddie Murphy had soared to new comic heights during his run on the show by creating characters that viewers demanded more of, so Adam took the same approach, hitting the bull's-eye with Operaman, Cajunman, and Canteen Boy.

A sidewalk performer on West 57th Street in New York inspired Adam to create Operaman. This real-life version sang arias in the hope that passersby would drop money into his cup. Adam's incarnation became a fixture on the show's regular news spoof "Weekend Update," only his arias were not from classic operas but from current events. When then Vice-President Dan Quayle created a stir by blasting TV's Murphy Brown for her lack of family values, Operaman belted out his take on the situation with, "Enuffo! Enuffo!/Topico over exposo!"

Cajunman came about in a similarly random fashion. "My friends and I had gone to a restaurant and there was this Cajun guy in front of us who had a 'reserva-*tion*.' Later, I started doing as many '*tions*' as possible," Adam explained to *Seventeen*. In his thermal undershirt, red suspenders, and straw hat, Adam had another winning character. Fans in Louisiana even implored him to dress up as Cajunman and be the grand marshal of a parade! Like Operaman, Cajunman became a welcome addition to the "Weekend Update" desk, only instead of breaking into song, he would give one-word, multisyllable responses to the news anchor's questions. When Kevin Nealon inquired about Cajunman's romantic luck, he got back the short but concise answer, "Rejec*tion*."

Canteen Boy was a blast from Adam's past. "He's just like the boys I knew when I was growing up in the neighborhood. He's a silly kid who stayed in the Scouts too long," Adam once said.

In what may have been an early version of "The Chanukah Song," Adam performed a ditty called "The Christmas Song" as a cold opener for the December 11, 1993, show. He sang, "Santa don't like bad boys/Especially Jewish ones!" Adam's drop-dead impressions of famous rockers also fueled his popularity. Pearl Jam's Eddie Vedder, Guns 'n' Roses' Axl Rose, U2's Bono, and Bruce Springsteen were all parodied on the show.

It's almost a rite of passage for *Saturday Night Live* guys to dress up in drag at some point, and Adam got his chance as Lucy the Gap Girl, a sketch he performed with David Spade, costar of *Tommy Boy*, *Black Sheep*, and now a regular on TV's *Just Shoot Me*. The two comics shared an office, which meant David endured

Adam's messy habits, including graffiti on the desk, papers strewn about, and comedy videos and books tossed everywhere. But at least David had a good reading on his friend's humor. "It's a different kind of funny," he told *People*. "It's like smart, thought-out dumb."

On seasonal breaks from *Saturday Night Live*, Adam tested the Hollywood waters with supporting parts in films. Roles as Dink in *Shakes the Clown* and Carmine in *The Coneheads* proved forgettable, but *Airheads* and *Mixed Nuts* garnered some positive buzz. In *Airheads* he portrays Pip, the would-be rock star alongside Brendan Fraser (*George of the Jungle, The Mummy*) and good friend Steve Buscemi. One critic who panned the film lamented that Adam's talent was wasted in an underwritten role.

Not so in the Nora Ephron comedy *Mixed Nuts*. Originally, the script called for just a little bit of Adam in the role of the ukelele-playing Louie, but the part was expanded to take advantage of the comic's talent for scene-stealing. The self-penned love song "Grape Jelly," a highlight of the film, is vintage Adam. Steve Martin starred in the movie, and Adam found himself frozen with fear in the face of one of his idols. "Steve would ask me a question, and I would just look at his lips moving," Adam told *Enter-*

tainment Weekly. "Steve was like, 'It's okay, Adam. You can talk.'"

Saturday Night Live had long been Adam's dream, but after five years, he'd had enough. "I felt like I had started repeating myself," he said to a journalist. "I didn't want to do that. I wanted to get into growing as much as I could." And so, Operaman had performed his last aria. Adam announced that he wouldn't return for the fall season.

Leaving a hit series is always a risky move, but Adam made his decision with the knowledge that his popularity went beyond late night TV and small movie parts. His first comedy album had scored a minor radio hit with "The Thanksgiving Song," a ridiculous ode to turkey dinner that gobbled onto playlists. Adam sings about eating turkey in a "big brown shoe."

The holidays were rich fodder for Adam's songwriting skills, and his second album featured his biggest radio hit to date, "The Chanukah Song," a catchy ditty hilariously rhyming Chanukah with words like "yarmulke" and "funakah." The song rocked into the top ten of *Billboard*'s Hot 100 airplay chart, then returned the next year, scoring so many spins that over 16 million listeners heard Adam croon about Harrison Ford being a quarter Jewish. According to Adam, that's not too shabby! Instantly, radio programmers called it a "holiday standard." New York's Z-100 even broke all seasonal-song policies — just for Adam. Listener demand forced the station to play "The Chanukah Song" as often as it played Pearl Jam or Alanis Morissette!

With the combined momentum of *Saturday Night Live* success, temporary rock stardom, and a string of supporting roles in movies, Adam set off on his next adventure — conquering Hollywood.

Ironically, his first shot at the big time sent him back to the place where he just couldn't stay out of trouble . . . high school.

Living the Life of Adam Tip #4

Want to go for a totally Adam look? That's easy. Slip into a sports jersey and some casual jeans or warm-up pants. Next, throw on your favorite baseball cap and flip it to the back. Then lace up some hiking boots or sneakers. Now strike a pose. You're kicking back, Adam-style.

4
Back to the Principal's Office

**When Adam came back in 1994, he was the same
kid who had left in 1984.**
— *Michael Clemons, Manchester High School
Central*

The path from *Saturday Night Live* to big-screen stardom is hardly a road less traveled. The list of veterans who've taken the leap from weekly TV sketches to films is long and impressive: Dan Aykroyd, Chevy Chase, Bill Murray, Eddie Murphy, and Billy Crystal. Given his status as one of the series' most popular cast members, Adam was standing at the lip of a career landslide. He was determined to take it all the way, but success wasn't guaranteed. Fellow *Saturday Night Live* player Mike Myers had a runaway hit with *Wayne's World*, yet Julia Sweeney crashed and burned with the disastrous *It's Pat: The Movie.*

For his first starring role, Adam made a strategic decision — to avoid cashing in on one of his popular sketch characters — Operaman didn't need his own movie, ditto for Cajunman. So with writing partner Tim Herlihy, Adam created a new lovable dope. The character — and the movie — would be called *Billy Madison*.

"I know it's gonna hurt if the movie eats it," Adam told *Entertainment Weekly* shortly before the film's release. "Billy's the closest I've come to playing myself. I feel so much pressure because I want it to be as good as it can be."

Adam test drives his material by giving his brother and close pals a peek. "Our friends are a tough laugh," explains cowriter Tim. "When we got laughs from them, we knew we were on the right track." Because the Sandler posse cracked up, *Billy Madison* got the go-ahead.

The title character is a rich goof-off who wastes away his days with two achievement-challenged buddies. Only when Billy's father threatens to turn over the family hotel business to a scheming weasel named Eric Gordon does Billy stop fooling around and get serious. He makes a winner-take-all bet with Papa Madison that he can repeat first grade through senior year in less than six months. Along the way, he wins friends of all ages, falls for a beautiful teacher, and gets his reputation sullied by his down-and-dirty nemesis, Eric. But by the closing credits, Billy snares the biggest prizes of all — respect from his family and the love of a terrific woman.

Behind-the-Scenes Exclusive

Tamra Davis directed *Billy Madison*, and this young filmmaker knows how to direct a comedy. Chris Rock's *CB4* is on her résumé, plus *Guncrazy*, which starred Adam's future leading lady Drew Barrymore. In addition to great movies, Tamra has directed such hot music videos as Hanson's "MMMbop" and Tatyana Ali's "Boy You Knock Me Out" featuring Will Smith. She's also married to Beastie Boys member Mike D — a good friend of Adam's. "They have a similar comic taste," Tamra remarks. "They keep getting older, but their audiences are getting younger. Adam and Mike laugh about that."

There was plenty to laugh about regarding *Billy Madison*, too. "We had a really good time," Tamra confirms. "When I do a comedy, I want to have a great time while I'm working. If Adam does a scene and I'm all stressed out or he's all stressed out, it doesn't feel like we're making a comedy. That's why I totally support the comedian to make sure his jokes get across. When Adam has the freedom to make sure it's exactly the way he needs it to be, that's when the movie works."

Entering the world of Adam can take some

getting used to, as Tamra quickly discovered. The script indicated that Billy has two loser friends who spend most of the movie beached on his pool deck, so Tamra logically assumed that both guys would be Adam's age. The star, however, had another idea, which he decided *not* to share with Tamra in advance. So imagine her surprise when the much older Norm MacDonald (now star of his own ABC sitcom and also an ex-*Saturday Night Live* player) showed up on the set. "I was like, okay, that's the joke. Billy's friends are forty years old or something. This is the kind of thing you'd never really know until you get to know Adam!" Tamra laughs.

Adam enjoyed hanging out with the littlest cast members and sometimes their acting prowess surprised him. "These kids we're working with are unbelievable," Adam said during the shoot. "Every time this one kid opens his mouth we laugh. It surprises you. You don't expect these little kids to be so funny. They're better actors than a lot of pros I know. I'm getting intimidated by a bunch of third graders."

While Adam charmed the children, Tamra planned one big chaos scene after another. Billy's graduation parties after he passes each grade required a cast of almost five hundred. Everything from carnival rides to elephants were part of the soup. Tamra blocked out these interludes with keen precision. After all, working with children *and* animals is always unpredictable. And so is working with Adam. "A couple of times when we were shooting I called 'Cut!' and Adam and the kids just kept playing," Tamra says.

Generally, Adam sticks closely to a script, but he feeds off spontaneous inspiration as well. Tamra devised a way to get the best of both worlds by shooting straight scripted scenes and following them with all-out crazy and goofy takes. Somewhere in between Tamra got the magic on film she needed. "That's the thing with comedy," she says, "you have to make it look like, 'Oh, ha, ha, I just thought of that.'"

It sure looked that way during the field trip scene when a little boy is ashamed to face the other kids because he wet his pants. To the rescue comes everyone's favorite overgrown elementary student . . . Billy Madison! He splashes water all over himself and announces that only the coolest kids wet their pants. Suddenly the whole class is lined up to board the bus, and all of them have wet their pants!

The movie's theme of going back to school must have been irresistible because Adam returned to his own Manchester High School Central shortly after *Billy Madison* wrapped. Since graduation, he's always reached out to the school when asked, but this time he stopped in just to say hello — and brought along a small film crew. He met with old teachers and familiar faces, gave time to starstruck students, signed autographs in the cafeteria, and visited classrooms to talk about his career.

Mr. Clemons, now an assistant principal but in Adam's day a U.S. government teacher, recalls the visit for two reasons. First, there was one faculty member who was less than thrilled to see the class clown of Central High return in triumph. "Mr. Blanchard didn't like Adam at all," says Mr. Clemons. "He told me, 'You take him around. I don't want to have anything to do with Adam Sandler.'" Guess he still held a grudge!

The second reason for Mr. Clemons' memory of his former student's visit is that a character in *Billy Madison* is named after him! "Adam wouldn't tell me in advance who it was," Mr. Clemons says. "He told me to go to the movie and see for myself." The sight wasn't pretty. Billy and his nutty sidekicks Frank and Jack light fire to a bag of poop and leave it on the front porch of old man Clemons, who stomps it out wearing only his underwear as the three goons cackle in the bushes. "This guy was scrawny," Mr. Clemons, the original, laughs. "I said to myself, 'Thanks a lot, Adam.'"

While audiences of all ages loved the movie, film critics didn't. They trashed it big-time. "Friends don't let friends make movies like this," one reviewer spat. But all the media hissing was drowned out by the laughter coming from packed theaters. *Billy Madison* opened at number one and went on to gross over $25 million. For a film modestly budgeted at $10 million, that translates to a nice little moneymaker.

Incredibly, that was only the beginning of *Billy Madison*'s success. On video, its popularity soared. College students all over the country began to host "Billy Nights." Adam sees the frenzy firsthand on his comedy tours and reports back to Tamra. "He loves that movie, and he's really excited that the film has grown in appreciation and popularity," she says. "Critics were so quick to dismiss it in the beginning, so Adam feels fairly vindicated now, not only because of where he is but because the movie still retains a huge audience. People love *Billy Madison*."

More important, they love Adam Sandler.

Living the Life of Adam Tip #5

Tired of Sloppy Joes at the school cafeteria? Here's something for the lunch lady's suggestion box: Serve up New York's famous Stage Deli Adam Sandler Sandwich. It's got Nova Scotia salmon, sturgeon, lettuce, tomato, and onion.

5
Don't Worry, Be Happy

One of Adam's all-time favorite films is the 1980 golf spoof *Caddyshack*, a comedy classic that stars *Saturday Night Live* hall-of-famers Bill Murray and Dan Aykroyd. Adam has seen the flick hundreds of times and often cites it as career inspiration, so it's no surprise that his next movie would focus on that sport. The fact that Adam enjoys golfing with his father in Florida might also have something to do with the theme.

Working with Tim Herlihy again, Adam co-scripted another laugh-out-loud comedy, *Happy Gilmore*. This one was about a radical-rage dude who can't skate well enough to earn a pro hockey slot but *can* drive a golf ball far enough to earn a PGA tour spot — especially when he needs the dough to help Grandma out of IRS trouble. But Happy's over-the-top behavior has no place in the sophisticated world of golf, hence, the film's tag line: "He doesn't play golf . . . he destroys it."

The slapstick farce features a dynamite cast. *Saturday Night Live*'s Kevin Nealon shows up, plus Carl Weathers (Apollo Creed from the *Rocky* movies) as an ex-golf pro whose wooden hand (a mean alligator ate his real one) gets some unintended abuse from the hapless Happy. Adam's buddy Allen Covert is on-screen as Otto, the homeless caddy. There's even an unbilled cameo by Adam's pal Ben Stiller as a nursing home orderly who terrorizes poor Grandma.

But the real scene-stealer is *The Price Is Right* host, old-timer Bob Barker. He's paired with Happy at a celebrity golf tournament, but the matchup goes sour when Happy suffers a rotten playing day. Suddenly the putting partners start throwing blows until an all-out fight to the finish ensues. Happy flattens Bob Barker on the green and cracks, "The price is wrong!" Just when Happy thinks the battle is over, Barker pulls some fast moves and cleans Happy's clock, pro-boxer style. The scene is a favorite among fans, many of whom admit watching it over and over again. No wonder Adam and Bob beat out some stiff competition to grab the 1997 MTV Movie Award for "Best Fight."

After its release, *Happy Gilmore* needed more than Otto to caddy the box office bucks. Adam's second starring vehicle took in almost $40 million at the theaters and enjoyed phenomenal video success. It's still a tough rental to find; folks can't get enough of Happy. The fan response prompted theater owners to decorate Adam with a ShowEast Award for Comedy Star of the Year. This was a treat, if only because Adam's mother could appreciate the praise, too. "*Happy Gilmore* is one of the first things I've done that my mother will watch and go, 'That was nice!'" Adam told the *Chicago Tribune* shortly after the movie opened. "When my mother sees half my stuff, she shrieks. But this will be nice for her."

Judy Sandler may well have "shrieked" over Adam's next film, the rough-and-tumble action flick *Bulletproof*. In fact, it's not regarded as a typical Adam movie. This was strictly an acting gig, a chance for Adam to experiment with action and drama, as well as to work with childhood hero James Caan. Sharing scenes with this movie great was bittersweet. "When I was a kid, my grandma used to say, 'You remind me of James Caan.' And I used to tell her, 'I'm gonna work with him one day. Maybe he'll play my dad.' I wish she could have seen this," he told the on-line *Mr. Showbiz*.

Adam plays a criminal, Archie Moses, who doesn't realize that his new best friend is really an undercover cop. There's an accidental shooting, a bounty hunt, turncoat cops, and car chases until the ultimate discovery of trust between two opposites. There's only one truly Adamesque moment, when his character sings "I Will Always Love You" in the shower!

But belting out that love ballad was good practice for his next project — a breakout movie that would take his career to a whole new level.

Living the Life of Adam Tip #6

Do you have a relative or family friend who's getting married soon? Here's a plan — sing Heatwave's "Always and Forever" at the reception, no matter how bad you sound. That's the song Adam crooned at a wedding for one of his friends. Just so you know, nobody screamed "Encore!"

6
A Little Music, a Little Romance

Humor and intellect make the best combination in a human being, and Adam's got them both.
— *Drew Barrymore, star of* The Wedding Singer

Even though Billy Madison won the teacher's heart and Happy Gilmore got his girl, critics were openly skeptical when word traveled that Adam's next movie would feature him as a bona fide romantic lead. What they soon discovered was that Adam was already considered dreamy by many female fans.

Says Christina Ferrari of *Teen People*, "Girls really like Adam. He seems like the kind of guy they could not only go out with, but be friends with. He's not conventionally handsome, but he's extremely appealing. In a recent Teen Research Unlimited poll, sense of humor is way at the top of the list of qualities girls look for in a boyfriend. They like guys who can make them laugh."

Adam was determined to make everybody laugh with his next movie, *The Wedding Singer*. Since his junior year in high school, *National Lampoon's Vacation* (starring fellow *Saturday Night Live* alumnus Chevy Chase) has been a favorite. "I remember going to movies when I was growing up in the eighties and you'd leave the theater with your friends, laughing and having a good time and feeling good. That's what we tried to do with the movie," he told *USA Today*.

The concept for his new project came to life like most of Adam's brilliant plans — out of brainstorm sessions with friends. "We wanted to do something set in the eighties, and we were batting around ideas," Tim Herlihy told *USA Today*. "People like to hear Adam sing, and I just got married. So it all came together." Subconsciously, the movie's theme may also owe its life to eleven-year-old Adam's singing debut at his sister's wedding. "I sang 'Yesterday' by Paul McCartney, and they started booing me," he quipped to the *Toronto Sun*. "I was taking away the focus. Apparently, the wedding was about those two getting married."

In *The Wedding Singer*, Adam plays Robbie Hart, a prospective bridegroom and aspiring songwriter who performs at weddings to pay the rent. His fiancée is Linda, a longtime girlfriend. Robbie and Linda are supposed to be the happy couple walking down the aisle, but when he shows up in a tux and she doesn't show up at all, the best wedding singer in town becomes the worst ever. In fact, while performing at another ceremony later on, the heartbroken Robbie sings Madonna's "Holiday" with such venom that he ends up in a fight with the bride's angry father! To play it safe, he gives up the wedding biz for bar mitzvahs.

Along the way, he befriends a waitress named Julia, who can't get *her* fiancé to plan their wedding. Julia enlists Robbie's help to get ready for the big day, and in the process the two secretly fall in love. Robbie really goes head over heels when he discovers that Julia's rich boyfriend is a cheat who doesn't deserve a girl so special. By movie's end, Robbie and Julia find true love on a plane heading to Las Vegas.

To pull off this romantic comedy, Adam needed the perfect leading lady. He found her in Drew Barrymore, the young actress who first captured America's hearts as the adorable Gertie in *E.T.* and is now a top favorite among teens for her roles in *Scream*, *Ever After*, and *Never Been Kissed*.

Drew is a sensational star who brings something unique to every role, and her portrayal of Julia in *The Wedding Singer* is no exception.

When Adam met Drew for the first time, he knew she was the right actress for the part. After grabbing a bite to eat with her and hanging out, Adam got together with his movie buddies to say, "Drew Barrymore is *cool*. She's really nice." Suddenly *The Wedding Singer* became a top priority for all concerned, including Drew. "I worked with Adam from the ground up," she informed *People Online*. "He told me about the concept, and we decided to do it together."

Drew has played many characters over the years, but Julia in *The Wedding Singer* struck a personal chord. "She's someone I aspire to be in a relationship, and I get closer to her every day. Robbie and Julia start off as friends. With friendship comes respect and honesty. Without those crucial cornerstones, lovers won't find safety and a sense of belonging."

Friendship is exactly what Drew found with Adam, a development that made for great chemistry during their romantic scenes. "Adam is so real and so organic and true in his performance," she gushed. In Adam's eyes, Drew is equally fabulous. "I love Drew. Everybody loves Drew. My mother loves her, and even the birds in my backyard love her," he said. In real life, the two on-screen lovers and offscreen friends enjoy hanging out and laughing together.

Even though Adam and Drew are the top stars in *The Wedding Singer*, they sometimes get upstaged by the clothes and the music. After all, the movie is a hilarious romp set in the glorious eighties. Mona May, duds designer for comedy hits like *Clueless* and *Romy and Michele's High School Reunion*, put all the cheesy costumes together. She dug deep for fashion tragedies like Michael Jackson's glitter glove, Madonna's "Borderline"-era rubber bracelets, Members Only jackets, and the ripped sweatshirt worn off the shoulder in vintage *Flashdance* style.

Some very brave costars don these relics, but Adam's real-life pal Allen Covert, who plays Sammy, endured the worst. "I was a walking ad for the eighties," Allen says. "I had shoulder pads, sleeveless shirts, mesh, parachute pants, pinkie rings — any crazy thing anyone ever saw in the eighties, they gave to me!" But Allen wasn't alone. Christine Taylor, best known for her dead-ringer turn as Marcia in *The Brady Bunch Movie*, put on lots of "Material Girl" wear for her role as Holly, Julia's Madonna-worshiping best friend.

Adam didn't mind Robbie's clothes, but Robbie's long hair was another matter. "That wig was not fun," he admitted to *People Online*. "They had to put that wig on me every day. I ripped it off a few times, and they yelled at me because that rips the netting or something. It costs money. But they never charged me because I would stare them down. That's my technique!"

The hairstyle may have reminded Adam of his own hair back in his Manchester High School Central days. "My dad used to tell me, 'You know, you got to get a haircut,' and I'd say, 'What is the matter with that old man? Doesn't he know how cool I look?' But looking back at the prom pictures, I feel bad for every girl."

There is one aspect of *The Wedding Singer* that no cast members complained about — the music. The movie boasts a fierce sound track of eighties-era hits from the Police, Bruce Springsteen, Hall & Oates, David Bowie, and Huey Lewis and the News. "It's as though somebody made you a good mixed tape," Drew told *People Online*. "We all listened to the album, and we were just moving and grooving and having a great time."

One of the songs they jammed to was Billy Idol's smash hit "White Wedding." Even more fun was nabbing the singer for a small part in the movie. It was a personal thrill for Adam. "We wrote him into the script, 'Billy Idol does this, Billy Idol does that,' and sent it to him, and then he said, 'All right, I'll do it,' and we're like, 'Yeah!'" Adam told the *Edmonton Sun*. What he didn't know was that Billy Idol's *kid* had already closed the deal. "I have an eight-year-old son, and he loves Adam, so now I'm a god for doing this," Billy said.

The Wedding Singer didn't just rely on veteran rockers to carry a tune. The film's stars took turns at the mike as well. Steve Buscemi was one of them. Adam's costar in *Airheads* shows up as a hopelessly bitter best man early in the film, then comes back to croon the old hit "True" at Robbie and Julia's wedding. Adam tries to create a cameo or supporting part for his pal Steve in every project, but this time things got out of control. "All of a sudden he became ridiculous," Adam explained. "We just started writing more stuff for him because one day on the set Buscemi was killing so hard, the crew was laughing."

Another laugh riot was Jon Lovitz, *Saturday Night Live* veteran and star of TV's *News Radio*. He appears in the film as a smarmy band singer auditioning to entertain at Julia's wedding. It's almost painful to watch Jon desecrate Kool and the Gang's "Ladies Night"! In all fairness though, Adam performs a few numbers that hurt, too, like the split-personality song "Somebody Kill Me," not to mention the airplane-cabin sappy love ballad "Grow Old with You."

Still, in the category of actor-turned-singer, most agree that elderly spitfire Rosie is the real scene-stealer. Played by Ellen Albertini Dow, Rosie takes voice lessons from Robbie so she can surprise her husband with a stirring version of "Til There Was You." After her touching serenade leaves no dry eye in the house, she gives the crowd a thrill by launching into the Sugarhill Gang classic "Rapper's Delight," one of the first hip-hop songs ever. This scene was played up heavily in *The Wedding Singer* trailers and stirred up advance excitement for the movie. But it did require some practice for Ellen to get jiggy with it. "She couldn't get the rap down at first," director Frank Coraci told *Entertainment Weekly*. "I got her to start dancing, and once she started moving, she nailed it perfectly. We started calling her Rappin' Rosie from Reseda."

Making the movie was a blast, but Adam, who's always hardest on himself, had another story for *People Online*. "I messed up every day on the set. I got a lot of stares from the other actors like, don't you know anything? This is a public apology to everybody I work with: You're in for a long day, but thanks for dealing with it."

No apology was necessary, especially when *The Wedding Singer* became a major hit, thanks in large part to Adam's performance. "You don't think of Adam Sandler as a romantic leading man, but he really won teenagers' hearts," *Teen People*'s Christina Ferrari says. "He allowed himself to be so vulnerable in that movie." For the first time in Adam's movie career, film critics became smitten as well. The *Los Angeles Times* noted that "Robbie represents a drastic change of pace for the usually abrasive Sandler, who emerges as a surprisingly appealing romantic lead."

The studio knew that Adam's latest vehicle was a potential smash and worked like gangbusters promoting it. In October 1997, three months ahead of the film's February release, the company sent out an elaborate wedding invitation from a couple named Michelle and Andrew, announcing their marriage at a conference for movie theater owners in Atlantic City. Most in attendance thought the stunt was some kind of gimmick, but it turns out the couple was for real — and so was the wedding. The true jaw-dropping moment came when Adam took the stage to lead the band!

The publicity machine didn't stop there. The studio sponsored a nationwide karaoke contest with sing-offs held in malls, clubs, and music shops. The final showdown happened in Orlando, with Adam on hand as a judge. The winner got $5,000 in studio recording time to make a rock-and-roll dream come true.

At the postscreening party held at the China Club in New York, Madonna showed up to give the movie a boost, no doubt because her record label, Maverick Records, issued the sound track. Adam, Drew, Jon Lovitz, and Conan O'Brien all partied late into the night.

The Wedding Singer eventually earned $80 million in ticket sales, making it one of the top

20 films of 1998, an achievement Adam antici-
pated since the romantic comedy opened on
Valentine's Day weekend. "Those two are going
to go together like a hamburger with a bun," he
told *People Online*. Not stopping with a box office smash, Adam and Drew also took home
1998's MTV Movie Award for "Best Kiss." Even
though he'd turned down an offer to host the
show (pal Ben Stiller stepped in to do the honors), Adam attended what is always an unpredictable ceremony. In his acceptance speech, he
thanked a sixth-grade girlfriend for his kissing
technique!

The Wedding Singer sent Adam's popularity
through the roof. His portrayal of Robbie Hart
revealed a sweet quality that had been down-
played in his earlier films. But for those who
know him well, it was hardly a revelation. Because the real Adam is loved by all.

Living the
Life of Adam
Tip #7

Feel like calling up a friend? Don't start off the
conversation with a boring "Hello." Sing a crazy
song, imitate someone else's voice, or play a silly
joke. That's what Adam does when he burns up
the telephone lines!

7
Phi Beta Sandler

**When the guys were at his house, we'd call it Phi
Beta Sandler.**
— *Christine Taylor, Adam's costar in*
The Wedding Singer

By the time *The Wedding Singer* opened to
box office fanfare, Adam had established a
tight-knit "boys' club" of NYU comrades who
worked together and played together. Adam and
company represent a new Hollywood guard —
young lions who make films with simple plots
and big laughs. Cool dudes with dough, they're
living a fantasy by making the kinds of movies
they loved to watch while growing up.

These guys have carved out a successful niche
for themselves in a tough industry. They're not
interested in rebellion, just dedicated to positive
vibes and having a good time. In a way, they're
similar to the young techno cowboys who banded

Adam Sandler *is* The Waterboy! This movie, which got dissed in nearly every review, went on to earn over $150 million. Not too shabby!

Touchstone Pictures/Shooting Star

As the team's "water distribution engineer," Bobby Bousher, Adam wins the respect of Coach Klein, who's played by Henry Winkler.

Retro Sandler: Back in the early '90s, Adam teamed with Brendan Fraser and Steve Buscemi in a comedy called Airheads.

Always the comedian—these shots from Adam's 1984 Manchester High School Central senior yearbook spotlight his comic ways.

Adam—shown here circa 1983 (left) and 1984 (right)—was voted class comedian.

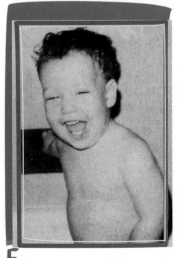

Adam Sandler
S.C. Del. 2-4, L.A. 3, L.G. 3, Bsktb. 1, 3.
Life is like a bowl of punch: It has a wang
to it. B.W., D.L., M.D. T.B. '84

Even as a toddler, Adam was all about getting laughs.

A true child of the '80's, Adam's style reveals glimpses of his future Wedding Singer character, Robbie Hart.

Globe Photos

In **The Wedding Singer**, Adam played Robbie Hart, a down-on-his-luck bridegroom who becomes bitter after getting dissed at the altar. But he eventually wins the heart of . . .

New Line Cinema/Shooting Star

. . . the lovely and lively waitress, Julia— portrayed with spunk by Drew Barrymore. **The Wedding Singer** is credited as the first Adam Sandler movie to appeal to girls as well as boys.

A couple in real life? No—but Drew and Adam did make happy faces at the movie's premiere. As well they should have, **The Wedding Singer** was a huge hit, grossing over $80 million.

Bruce Macaulay/Shooting Star

Adam played the title role in 1995's Billy Madison, about a young heir forced to repeat all twelve years of school within six months, in order to control the family business.

Happy Gilmore— again playing a not-too-bright character who wins in the end— was another surprise hit.

Universal/Shooting Star

And he sings! Famous for "The Chanukah Song" and "Lunchlady Land," Adam pens these ditties himself. They're often on the soundtracks of his movies, and on his comedy CDs.

Just like his movie characters, he wins big! At the 1998 MTV Movie Awards, Adam picked up a prize for "Best Onscreen Kiss" with Drew Barrymore in The Wedding Singer. It wasn't his first MTV Movie Award. In 1995, he won "Best Fight Scene," in Happy Gilmore.

Big Daddy is Adam's newest movie. He plays a sweet slacker named Sonny forced to accept grown-up responsibilities when a little boy gets dumped on his doorstep.

The role of Julian—the little boy in Big Daddy— is played by six-year-old identical twins Cole and Dylan Sprouse, who rotate scenes. This is Cole with Adam.

together to revolutionize the computer industry in Silicon Valley. Only this group is changing the movie industry!

The life of a Hollywood young lion is not exactly complicated. A typical day might include watching football or basketball on a huge television, playing video games and air hockey, and eating pumpkin pancakes at Hugo's in West Hollywood. It might sound like a day at the beach, but Adam just makes it look that way. "He's one of the hardest workers in this industry, and he doesn't really take that much time off," Tamra Davis says. The *Billy Madison* director knows that on Planet Adam, funny business is serious business. By the time each movie wraps, he's hard at work on another.

What Adam brings to everything he does is integrity and thoughtfulness — a rare combination in Hollywood. For example, when ABC–TV's union members were on strike last fall, he refused to cross the picket line for a scheduled appearance on *Good Morning, America*. His decision created a minor panic, and network reps tried to convince Adam to honor his commitment. But the young lion wasn't swayed. Loyalty to the working class prevailed.

When he's not making movies, recording comedy albums, or touring to sold-out crowds, Adam enjoys just hanging out. Some comedians are low-key when the stage lights dim, but Adam is decidedly not. The Comic Strip's Lucien Hold says he's "the straw that stirs the drink" in any group — especially a roomful of guys. "He tells great jokes and loves to talk. Get ten guys together and there'd be few people they would enjoy spending an evening with more than Adam Sandler. Even though he's a major star and a multimillion-dollar man, you don't feel threatened."

Mr. Hold, who spent countless hours with Adam during his comedy club days, also reveals there's a "bad boy" side to the star as well. "That would be his college shows and work with bands. For boys, it just indicates that he's a guy's guy. For girls, he's got a little bit of naughtiness, and that makes him even more lovable. He's truly a ladies' man . . . like a rock star. It's got to be awkward for him. I suspect that he'll settle down eventually, but not at the moment."

In fact, Adam almost marched down the aisle with Margaret Ruden, a cosmetics company executive he proposed to in 1995. "I just popped it out," Adam admitted in an interview for *Mademoiselle*. "I feel loved to the point where I know she wants me to be happy, and I wanted to make sure she knew I loved her."

The romance did not last, however. But even today, the former couple remain friends.

Newly single, Adam reportedly moved on to

romance one of the industry's hottest young stars, Alicia Silverstone of *Clueless* and *Batman and Robin* glory. *People* magazine reported that they dated in 1996, when she was 19 and he 29. Adam never publicly admitted to it, nor did Alicia. The Batgirl of the nineties has always kept her love life under wraps. When rumors hit that Alicia's relationship with *Titanic* star Leonardo DiCaprio had hit an iceberg of its own, all she offered to *Vanity Fair* was a hollow, "I will not say anything about Leo." She was just as tight-lipped regarding Adam. No matter, talk of the love connection bandied about long enough to turn doubters into believers.

These days, Adam is with 24-year-old Jackie Titone, a former high school cheerleader who's now a model. They met at an exclusive Hollywood bash just before *The Wedding Singer* opened. Though usually intensely private about Adam's personal life, friends let it slip to the *New York Post* that he and Jackie are "totally in love." Adam proposed marriage and Jackie accepted — just one year after meeting. The big question on everyone's mind — will Adam sing at his own wedding?

Whether spending private time with that special someone or just hanging out with friends, one thing is certain — Adam is simply the nicest guy around. Former manager Barry Moss saw it firsthand. "He has an accessibility, a warmth, a *goodness*." It's a rare quality, one that compels people to reach out to him in times of trouble.

Manchester High School Central's Robert Schiavone remembers a young woman who did. She was hospitalized in intensive care, and her family got word to a teacher at Central that Adam Sandler was her favorite comedian. Once Adam learned of the situation, he called to wish his fan a speedy recovery and invited her to New York for a night on the town when she got well. When she recovered and took him up on his offer, Adam treated her to a great time. "That's the type of guy he is, and many people don't know that about him," Mr. Schiavone says.

Sometimes, tragically, Adam *can't* help a person in need. Talented Chris Farley, a friend from *Saturday Night Live* days and the crazy school-bus driver in *Billy Madison*, was one pal who fell beyond reach. "Like a lot of comedians, Chris had his high ups and low downs," Adam told the *Toronto Sun*. "When he was down, I tried to get him up again, but it wouldn't always work."

Chris suffered from alcohol and drug addiction, which ultimately killed him in 1997. His funeral was held in the comedian's native Madison, Wisconsin, at Our Lady Queen of Peace Roman Catholic Church. Adam was there, fighting tears as he sought the comforting embrace of *Saturday Night Live* veteran Dan Aykroyd.

"A Clown's Prayer" graced the back of the printed program: "Dear Lord, as I stumble through this life, help me to create more laughter than tears."

For Adam, losing a friend like Chris brought on many tears. "I have never gone through this before," he told *USA Today*. "I had grandparents pass away, and that hurts a lot. But that's natural. This is an unnatural death. And I can't stop thinking about it."

Moving past the pain, Adam found a way to move on and pay tribute to Chris as well. "I like thinking of him. I like thinking that he's listening, and I like trying to make him laugh."

Somewhere in heaven, Chris Farley is smiling down.

Living the Life of Adam Tip #8

Do the people around you seem bored and restless? Write a silly poem that makes no sense at all and recite it aloud. That's what Adam did for the 8,000 extras who showed up to play the wild crowd for the big Bourbon Bowl finale in *The Waterboy*.

8
Splish Splash

I had no idea what a fine young man Adam
Sandler is. I would be proud to call him my son,
but I would like to emphasize that I am not old
enough to be Adam's mother.
— *Kathy Bates, star of* The Waterboy

What Happy Gilmore did for golf, Bobby
Boucher was about to do for football —
turn the game upside down, that is. To follow up
The Wedding Singer, Adam and his crew decided
to get stupid again. The perfect vehicle was a
movie about a sheltered mama's boy from Louisiana swamp country who can tackle Godzilla if
mad enough.

Adam conceived the premise for *The Waterboy*
and collaborated with old friend and writing
partner Tim Herlihy on the screenplay, just as
they'd done on *Billy Madison* and *Happy Gilmore.*
When the story line calls for supreme doofus be-

havior, a script needs that special touch only Adam can provide.

The Waterboy casts Adam as the sweet but dim-witted Bobby Boucher, a home-schooled, socially sheltered young man who takes great pride in his job as waterboy for a college team. This guy takes his H_2O seriously, creating elaborate filters and dispensers to make sure the water is fresh and pure when the team drinks it. Years of abuse by the players and even the coach hasn't fazed him. After all, Bobby's mama explained how his father had died of dehydration in the desert, so he knows how important water is! Despite Bobby's dedication, the team's hard-nosed Coach Red Beaulieu fires him for distracting the team with his goofy ways. This move sets off a chain of events that the coach soon regrets.

Bobby volunteers to serve as waterboy for the worst college team in the country. In short order, he wins the favor of the Mud Dogs' beleaguered Coach Klein, who's just about one field goal away from a breakdown — but in his own way, wise and compassionate. Instead of taking abuse from the bullies on the team, Coach Klein encourages Bobby to stand up for himself, to fight back. And that's exactly what he does. When Bobby uses all his pent-up rage as adrenaline fuel, he's suddenly the kind of take-no-prisoners tackling machine that can mow down even the toughest defensive line. Coach Klein is amazed, sees Bobby as a secret weapon for the team, and convinces him to suit up and play ball.

But Bobby's courage extends to going against his mama's wishes. She's against him actually *playing* the sport, so he begins his new life in secret — going to college, becoming a football wonder, and even dating his longtime crush, Vicki Vallencourt.

The Waterboy has it all — sports adventure, a live-your-dreams message, quirky romance, and the sentimental journey of a boy's unwavering loyalty to his mother. The driving force behind the movie is, of course, the laugh-out-loud funny parts — and there are many.

One of the biggest crowd-pleasing gags is the slam dunk on poor old Professor, who becomes body carpet after he questions the scientific wisdom of Mama. More howls come when Coach Klein tells Bobby that Gatorade is better than water, just to get him stirred up enough to tackle the opposing team like nobody's business. As the movie's tag line warns, "You can mess with him. But don't mess with his water."

But Bobby isn't the only character to keep fans in stitches. Mama Boucher has her own memorable moments. Who can forget the barbecued baby alligators she serves up for Bobby's afternoon lunch date with Vicki?

Surprisingly, Kathy Bates, the Oscar-winning actress who portrays Mama Boucher, came close to passing on the role. "I almost didn't even want to read the script," the *Titanic* star told *The New York Times*. "I thought, it's not what I usually do. But I read it because my niece is an Adam Sandler fan. I decided to do it, and I ended up having a blast."

Another actress who had a great time was Fairuza Balk, best known for her starring role in the witchy thriller *The Craft*. Fairuza sizzles in her role as Bobby's main squeeze, Vicki Vallencourt. "I thought it would be a gas to work on this film because Adam is a very sweet, sensitive guy. He's very with it and very together. He doesn't miss a beat," she says.

The Waterboy marks Fairuza's first role in a comedy — and her first encounter with the high-energy atmosphere from a nearly all-male cast and crew. She enjoyed the zany mood that prevailed throughout filming. From the first take to the last, Fairuza found making movies with Adam and company to be a guaranteed good time.

It turns out that Adam was equally impressed. He praised Fairuza in a recent *E-Online* cyber chat. "She's really funny, a really nice girl, very smart, and a strong actress. Every time she comes on-screen, you're glad she's there."

Adam was also pleased that Henry Winkler,

best known for his role as the leather-jacketed "Fonz" on *Happy Days*, joined the cast. Adam and Tim wrote the Coach Klein role with Henry in mind. The actor's legendary TV persona even pops up in "The Chanukah Song." Henry had only great things to say during a recent appearance on MTV's *Loveline*. "Adam Sandler is brilliant. He is one funny guy."

Underneath all that fun, however, there is serious work being done, a fact that didn't escape the notice of Henry, either. At his first official read-through as Coach Klein on *The Waterboy* set, the *Happy Days* star was captivated by Adam's laser focus. "I watched him as he heard the material being read, and Adam was in complete charge of every joke. He knew if it worked or if it didn't."

But sometimes Adam wasn't sure how to *pronounce* the joke — case in point, the Cajun gibberish of Farmer Fran, Coach Klein's funny-talking assistant. "I thought *The Waterboy* was a great script, but I couldn't understand my part," remembers Blake Clark, who brings the gum-flapping fool to life in a hilarious performance. What made things even more difficult — sometimes even Adam, who actually wrote the nonsensical lines, couldn't help Blake with the translations!

Surprises like that are expected on movie

sets, but *The Waterboy* had more than its share. Riding a lawn mower (Bobby's preferred method of transportation) at a snail's pace was easy, but taking it for a spin after Vicki Vallencourt gave it a speedway-style tune-up was another situation altogether. In fact, Adam's first test *drive* on the newly charged-up mower almost turned into a test *crash*. At one point, he raced past the camera like an out-of-control speed demon, and the sight of him cracked up the crew.

Adam had another shocker in store when he, Fairuza Balk, and Kathy Bates boarded the fan boat that delivers Bobby to the Bourbon Bowl just in the nick of time. The adventurous Kathy deep-sixed the idea of a stunt double and decided to drive the swamp vehicle herself. Once Adam and Fairuza were seated, the director yelled "Action!" Kathy started the boat on its way, but the water vessel had more power than she ever imagined, and the three stars took off like a rocket. Luckily, there were no injuries — but there *was* a lesson: leave the souped-up lawn-mower and swamp-boat driving to the pros.

Yet another on-set surprise came from Mother Nature. During filming, the DeLand, Florida, location was hit by a tornado. Thankfully, nobody was seriously hurt, but the town's residents suffered major property damage. True to his spirit, Adam helped organize a clothing-and-cash drive from all the actors and production staff. Just like his lovable movie characters, Adam has a big heart — a fact that's no secret in Hollywood.

But even nice guys have to get down to some necessary roughness on occasion, which is exactly what Adam had to do for the football scenes. "I had the best time making this. It was fun pretending I was tough," he told *People*. "In real life I'm nothing. I have no fighting skills. If you wanted to hit me, I wouldn't do anything about it. I'd just cry like a baby."

Thankfully, it was only make-believe. "Playing [football] at age thirty-two, I found out I'm more brittle than I thought I was," Adam says. That's why stunt coordinator Allan Graf, who choreographed the game plays for Cuba Gooding Jr. in *Jerry Maguire*, was called in to protect Adam and the other actors from bumps and bruises. Because the film was shot during football's off-season, casting calls attracted some actual pros. Players from the Florida State team, always a major force in the annual battle for the national title, made the final cut.

When an overeager Adam decided to don a helmet and mix it up with the big boys, Allan Graf had his work cut out for him. The real players, worried about colliding too roughly with the multimillion-dollar funny man, found themselves falling all over the place.

At the end of the day, however, the football scenes were the real deal. Adding to the authenticity, aside from the college players, was a host of cameos by top names in the world of sports. Pittsburgh Steelers Coach Bill Cower, ESPN's Dan Patrick, and *Monday Night Football*'s Lynn Swan are just some of the big names in the film.

In the stands for the crowd-packed games were 8,000 extras, most of them students and residents from the DeLand area. To beef up any empty rows or spaces between people, production assistants put cardboard body cutouts in place, an old movie trick that works in a pinch. Shooting a film is long and tedious work, so the extras were required to sit in the stands for hours. But visits from Adam and Henry Winkler helped pass the time. The girls in the bleachers were especially attentive, always on the lookout for Adam.

Some lucky high schoolers actually got to spend memorable time with Adam. The extras who are part of the pep rally scene were rewarded with a meet-and-greet/let's-hang-out session with the star after the day's shooting wrapped up.

The Waterboy went on to become Adam's biggest hit to date, exceeding all expectations. The movie racked up more than $145 million in ticket sales, a figure that put it in the top five of all films released in 1998. For Adam, the whizbang success meant a great deal because *The Waterboy* is the funny, feel-good type of movie he loved going to as a teenager. "I really like this movie," he said. "We made it so fans could have an hour and a half of, hopefully, laughs. Or at least smiles."

Mission accomplished. But no matter how much loot his flick took in at the box office, Adam still chided his mother for taking her senior citizen friends to his movies. "They pay only half price," he teased her. "Get some younger friends so I can get some business, Ma."

Living the
Life of Adam
Tip #9

Do you want to be cool in true Adam Sandler style? That's easy to do. Stay dedicated to the people you love and look out for them. Your family and good friends should always come first.

9
The Big Daddy
of Comedy

*The relationship that develops between my sons
and Adam in this movie is beautiful. It's not just
what you see on the screen. It really happened.*
*— Melanie Sprouse, mother of child actors
Cole and Dylan*

Even before the stunning success of *The Waterboy*, Adam had already signed to star in
another project. Typically, a movie takes three
months to shoot and three months to edit. For
someone like Adam, who is arguably one of the
hardest workers in the business, it's not uncom-
mon to have a movie in the can, a movie in the
making, and a movie in development.

This new vehicle, scripted by Steve Franks,
was originally titled *Guy Gets Kid*. Tim Herlihy
gave the screenplay a major rewrite to focus
on Adam's strengths, and soon the hot project
was rechristened *Big Daddy*. Almost immedi-

ately, buzz on the film became electric. ADAM SANDLER PLAYS INSTANT FATHER TO FIVE-YEAR-OLD. That's a can't-miss concept if ever there was one! *Teen People*'s Christina Ferrari agrees. "Combining Adam's little boy qualities and his brand of humor with a *real* little boy is just a huge comic smash."

Adam's acting turn in *Big Daddy* is an ambitious move. Like his role in *The Wedding Singer*, he's slightly more serious in this film, which really tugs at the heartstrings. Adam plays Sonny, a toll taker at a bridge who, like most of Adam's characters, is driving everyone around him bonkers as he searches for his place in the world. One day a five-year-old boy shows up on the doorstep of the apartment Sonny shares with his best friend, a slick corporate mover who's out of the country on business. In short order, Sonny realizes that the boy's name is Julian, that Julian's father is Sonny's best friend, and that not being able to reach his roommate means Sonny will have to care for the boy temporarily.

Parenthood doesn't come easy to overgrown kid Sonny, a situation that makes for a big laugh ratio. Because Sonny has no experience raising a child, he simply teaches Julian to act like him, which means everything from tripping in-line skaters in the park to skipping much-needed baths. Julian eventually becomes the stinkiest boy in his kindergarten class and is taunted by the other kids. Sonny never intended for Julian to suffer hurt feelings, so he sets out to improve himself and the boy.

One funny scene has Sonny trying to convince Julian that bathing is fun, so Sonny dresses up as the boy's favorite action figure, Scuba Steve, flippers and all. The script calls for Julian to ask "What does Scuba Steve wear when he goes bowling?" Sonny thinks for a moment and erupts with, "I think he wears *blippers!*"

When Sonny learns the real reason Julian's mother dropped him off at his dad's house — she's dying of cancer — he tries to adopt the boy, but that plan falls through. In the end, Julian is lovingly taken in by Sonny's best friend, the boy's natural father who steps up, along with his fiancée, to raise the child he never knew about. Actor/comedian Jon Stewart and *George of the Jungle*'s Leslie Mann star as the couple.

Sonny's lady love in *Big Daddy* is played by Joey Lauren Adams of *Chasing Amy* fame, but the real love affair in the movie exists between Sonny and Julian. The little kid teaches the big kid a lot about life, and by the end of the film Sonny is a goof-off no more. He earns the respect of his father, the love of a special woman, and the lifelong friendship of a child.

Behind-the-Scenes Exclusive

Finding two real little boys to alternate in the role of Julian proved to be no small endeavor. Just ask Melanie Sprouse, mommy/manager of Cole and Dylan, the lucky identical twins who landed the most-sought-after child's role of the year. Though only six years old, Cole and Dylan are old pros in Hollywood. At six months, they were cast in the family sitcom *Grace Under Fire*. That show enjoyed a five-year run, so the boys practically grew up on television. When agent Judy Savage called about the *Big Daddy* audition, Melanie harbored initial reluctance, "But something in the back of my mind told me to go for this one. I've always liked Adam and admired the creativity in his work. I wanted my boys to get this part."

Early on, the producers hadn't decided on the kind of child they wanted for the role of Julian, so it was only necessary for Cole to attend callbacks. Like Mary Kate and Ashley Olsen, who traded off in the role of Michelle on *Full House*, Cole and Dylan would eventually do the same on *Big Daddy*. Child labor laws limit the number of hours that kids can work, and because movie shoots often require long days, it helps when twins can share a role. That way the film stays on schedule.

From June to September of 1998, Melanie helped prepare her son for the many auditions.

The producers sent script samples via fax, and some readings required up to nine pages of dialogue — a hefty amount for a six-year-old to memorize. But Melanie worked closely with Cole to help him learn the lines, and it paid off. On Cole's first day of first grade, Melanie got The Call summoning him to New York for a screen test with Adam. The California-based Sprouses were on the next plane.

Upon arrival, they spent the first day getting Cole a haircut and learning new dialogue pages. Next stop — Adam's penthouse suite in one of Manhattan's most exclusive hotels. Joining them were director Dennis Dugan (also behind the lens for *Happy Gilmore*) and Adam's long-time buddy and producer Jack Giarraputo. "It was very casual and nonintimidating," Melanie says. "We got to hang out with Adam."

Everything was fine until the hotel fire alarm started blasting in the middle of the screen test. Adam and company had to evacuate — and they were 45 floors up! "It turned out to be a drill, so we headed back up to the suite," Melanie says. "Actually, it was kind of funny. Pretty radical."

Melanie and Cole flew back to California to await word on the decision. When it finally came down, there was no time to dawdle. Cole had wowed Adam, Dennis, and Jack, and they wanted both boys on the New York set within 24 hours. Melanie packed enough clothes and sports equipment for the three-month shooting schedule and off they went!

Auditioning for the movie was serious business, but making it was an absolute blast. "I laughed more in four months than I have in my entire life," Melanie says. "It was like working in a comedy shop. Adam is hysterical."

The good times on *Big Daddy* never stopped, especially since the monster success of *The Waterboy* hit during the movie's shoot. Cole and Dylan attended the star-studded premiere with Adam. "It was fabulous," Melanie says. "Just to be surrounded by all that excitement made our working environment so positive. It was like watching someone win the marathon. I feel so grateful that I got to witness such camaraderie among coworkers. You usually don't get to see that. Adam's gang is made up of such casual, friendly people who work so well together. They're all old friends and have a wonderful history. That's why their movies really touch the hearts of audiences."

And the hearts of Cole and Dylan. When the boys were very young, Melanie made up a fairy tale about The Sandman, a special friend who leaves coin-shaped chocolate under the pillows of good children who keep their rooms clean, brush their teeth, and treat people with kindness. Adam's close friends call him The Sandman, and hearing this, Cole and Dylan began to think that Adam really *was* this fantasy figure they'd grown up believing in. Melanie confirmed it by giving Adam coin-shaped chocolates on the sly to hand out to the boys!

As if it wasn't enough to be The Sandman to Cole and Dylan, Adam made himself an honorary uncle, too. He spent a lot of time with his young costars, allowing the boys to strum on his guitars, buying them remote-controlled cars, and sharing his popcorn. "He was like a big kid," Melanie says. "He's a wonderful, gentle human being." In turn, the twins would draw Adam pictures, make him holiday cards, and help their mom bake special treats for him. The kids also loved playing pinball on the vintage machine used as an on-set prop for Sonny's apartment. Between breaks in shooting, everybody took a turn at the game, keeping records of the highest scores.

At Christmastime, Adam told Melanie, "You know, I really want to get the boys something special. I'm trying to think of what I can get them." Later, on the second to last day of shooting, Adam told Melanie he'd purchased the pinball machine for Cole and Dylan and would have it shipped to California. "I hope you've got room for it," Adam said, smiling.

Making a feature-length movie is a long, intense process. Friendships form fast, and everybody begins to feel like family. That's especially true on the set of an Adam Sandler film. "We spent four months away from home," Melanie says, "and my boys never complained. They looked forward to every single day. I saw how much these guys cared about us, and I feel really grateful for the experience."

But filming eventually came to an end. Dylan and Cole had to say good-bye to Uncle Adam. They didn't want to let him go and parting was tough, but the little boys and their big-kid friend still stay in touch. Adam's trademark thoughtfulness comes through with phone calls and surprise packages. The twins have even set up a lunch with Adam and invited him to attend one of their T-ball games.

"I am the proudest mother in the whole world," Melanie says. "It's such a great movie. I haven't seen anything like this. It's got every element and every type of character. There are parts where you're going to bend over laughing and parts where you're going to cry. It's really touching."

So is the real-life relationship that developed between Adam and the twins. Everyone in Adam's circle agrees that his ability to interact with children is one of his greatest gifts.

Future fatherhood may be uncertain, but future laughs are guaranteed. Adam Sandler is one Big Daddy destined to stay on top of the Hollywood comedy heap.

Living the
Life of Adam
Tip #10

Do you have a dream? Then go after it the way Adam Sandler did his own. First, *really* decide to do it, then stay focused, work as hard as you can, and don't allow the negativity of others to impact confidence in yourself or your goal. You'll find success . . . just like Adam.

Epilogue:
Last Laugh

Adam was always the kid to be taken out and told, "You're not going to succeed." But no matter what you told him, it didn't register. If he had listened to his teachers, he never would have gotten anywhere.
— Mel Gordon, former NYU drama teacher/student counselor

"We all know what it's like to be a bit of a loser," Jack Giarraputo, Adam's producer buddy, told *Newsweek*. "I think our movies give kids hope." So should the turn of events in Adam's life — proof positive that hard work, laser focus, and positivity pay off big-time. Adam approached his success one step at a time, the building blocks for a long career.

Teen People's Christina Ferrari likens him to Bill Murray, who, when Adam's age, played the goof, got the girl, and laughed on to a brilliant career. "Women will always like the little boy quality in Adam, even as he gets older and the girls get older."

With *Big Daddy*, Adam's playing papa (always a can't-miss move with the ladies) and finally getting the star treatment he deserves. *Billy Madison*, *Happy Gilmore*, and *The Wedding Singer* were all released on President's Day weekend, a great place to be, but not the prime summer or holiday slot that a Tom Cruise or Harrison Ford picture demands. Though *The Waterboy* took its bow in November, that movie rowed in a few weeks short of the coveted Thanksgiving weekend debut.

Not the case with *Big Daddy*. The latest Adam Sandler film was, from the get-go, positioned as a summer event. Translation — an A-list movie with mega advertising and promotional dollars behind it. In a season boasting the latest *Star Wars* saga, Episode I: *The Phantom Menace*, and Will Smith in *Wild Wild West*, that can only mean one thing: Adam Sandler has advanced to the head of the class. Indeed. He's the first actor in history to nab both the ShowEast and Sho-West awards for Comedy Star of the Year from theater owners.

Next up for Adam is *Little Nicky*, a father-son comedy with a twist. It's the first offering from Adam's two-picture, mega-million deal with New Line, the studio that released *The Wedding*

Singer. The premise of the second film hasn't been revealed. But so what? If a movie stars Adam Sandler, that's reason enough to put untold millions on the line.

And get ready for more — including a cartoon version of Adam. He's dreamed up an idea for a new kind of musical, but animated films can take years to produce, so a singing comic book version of Adam probably won't hit screens until sometime in the millenium. One thing is certain — it'll offer Adam the chance to write more silly songs and, the big-screen cartoon may be about Adam's real life.

There's also the possibility of a baseball film in his future. After all, the sports theme sure made heroes out of Happy and Bobby, and one of Adam's fondest childhood memories is a Knicks game at Madison Square Garden.

Some wonder if Adam intends to follow in the footsteps of Robin Williams and Jim Carrey by taking on more serious roles. "Will he continue this adorable, geeky persona or do more ambitious things? No one knows but him," muses Glenn Kenny of *Premiere*. One possible project is a more somber role in a biopic of legendary crooner Dean Martin. Adam might play Joey Bishop, an old-school comedian who, along with Dean, traveled in Frank Sinatra's famous Rat Pack.

Another possibility is music played for real —

not for laughs. Adam's comanager from yesteryear, Barry Moss, believes it could happen. Because he fools around with his singing so much, people don't realize how strong a vocalist Adam really is. "A long time ago we talked about doing a serious music album," Moss says. "He actually recorded a demo of songs, which I thought were really impressive. Adam could go into Broadway musicals — that would open up a whole new avenue. The sky's the limit."

Chris Rock agrees. "I think we're just getting started with the adventures of Adam," he predicted to *Entertainment Weekly*. Now there's an idea — Adam as superhero.

Faster than a complaining teacher.

More powerful then a jabbing film critic.

He can break box office records in a single weekend.

It's . . . Sandman!

Appendix:
The Essential Adam
Collection

Television

The Best of Saturday Night Live 1991
The Best of Saturday Night Live 1992
The Best of Saturday Night Live 1993

This compilation video series from StarMaker Video features some of Adam's classic moments from the show that launched him as a comic sensation. Priced less than ten bucks at some discount outlets.

Movies

Coneheads
Mixed Nuts
Airheads
Billy Madison
Happy Gilmore

Bulletproof*
The Wedding Singer
These films are now discounted videos — all less than twenty bucks, many less than ten. At press time, the initial video release of *The Waterboy* was priced exclusively for the rental market (about $100). Typically, the price drops to a consumer's budget within six months. On the Internet, www.reel.com is a good on-line source for new and used videos.

Comedy Recordings
Mixed Nuts: Original Motion Picture Soundtrack
They're All Gonna Laugh at You!*
What the Hell Happened to Me?*
What's Your Name?*
The Wedding Singer: Original Motion Picture Soundtrack
The Wedding Singer Volume 2: More Music from the Motion Picture
   All of Adam's comedy recordings are currently available on CD and cassette.

*Contains explicit language and adult humor. Please secure permission from a parent or legal guardian before renting or purchasing.

Internet

www.adamsandler.com

There are enough cyber shrines to Adam on the World Wide Web to fill a universe, but this one is the *official* fan site. It's managed by Jack Giarraputo and Allen Covert, members of Adam's inner circle, so it includes behind-the-scenes photos, tidbits, special contests, and spontaneous chats. Bookmark it!

About the Author

Jon Salem earned a Master of Arts degree in American Studies with a concentration in popular culture from the University of Alabama. He cowrote the foreword to the 1997 reissue of Barbara Seaman's *Lovely Me: The Life of Jacqueline Susann* (Seven Stories Press) and has profiled actor-dancer-singer Gregory Hines for a Mississippi-based news weekly. Also a novelist, his first suspense thriller, *Remember September*, is set for release this fall from Pinnacle Books. Under the pseudonym Jona Jeffrey, he writes contemporary romance and romantic comedy.